Meditation
in
Christianity

Meditation in Christianity

Compiled by
The Himalayan International Institute
of Yoga Science and Philosophy

Contributing Editors:

Swami Rama
Pandit Usharbudh Arya, Ph.D.
Justin O'Brien, Ph.D.
Father William Teska
Reverend Lawrence Bouldin

Published by
The Himalayan International Institute
of Yoga Science and Philosophy
Honesdale, Pennsylvania

Library of Congress Catalog Card Number: 79-92042

ISBN: 0-89389-063-4

Copyright 1973, 1979
The Himalayan International Institute
of Yoga Science and Philosophy
Honesdale, Pennsylvania 18431

Contents

Introduction

From the beginnings of Christianity (and even earlier in the religious life of the people of Israel) there has been a tradition of meditation which persists to this day. It is the purpose of the present volume to explore this tradition.

Our reasons for selecting the articles to be included have been fourfold: First, we have attempted to present a view of the relationship of Christianity to other Eastern traditions in which there is a dominant emphasis on meditation. Historical evidence is presented, for instance, which points to the likelihood that Jesus and the fathers of the Christian faith were well acquainted with the ancient meditative disciplines. It is also shown how the purpose of meditation in Christianity became less important as the various modes of worship and dogma replaced the experiential knowledge of meditation as the basis of Christian belief.

A second intent of this volume is to examine the basis for meditation within the Bible itself. There has been a continuous, though often suppressed, tradition within the church which has found in the scriptures an esoteric guide to the practice of meditation as well as a source of hidden wisdom which becomes more fully apparent to aspirants as they progress along the spiritual path. This wellspring of spiritual truth has always nourished the great mystics and teachers of Christianity. It remains today the chief resource for persons who are seeking to unfold within themselves a greater awareness of the indwelling consciousness of Christ.

A third reason for this volume is to trace the history of a significant meditative tradition, within the church, a tradition which has spanned many centuries. From this much can be learned that will be of help to all who seek to establish a method of meditation based on Christian insights and goals.

And, finally, the present volume includes a discussion of some of the obstacles which stand in the way of successful meditation. Some of these are personal and require a change in the style and values of one's life; others are rooted in the narrowness of sectarianism and dogmatism in religion. But whatever the reason for them, as the hindrances to meditation are cleared away one will find the key which frees him from the bondage of ignorance and attachments of the earth, and it then becomes possible for him to experience the "new birth" of an expanded capacity to perceive and respond to the infinite consciousness which is God.

Meditation thus gives us hope for a future of peace on earth and for the attainment of brotherhood among men, for through meditation one rediscovers the essential unity of purpose which underlies the many approaches to realization of God.

LAWRENCE M. BOULDIN

Meditation
in Christianity

Swami Rama

Religion should not consist of mere intellectual conformity. The human mind is badly crippled by thinking that truth has already been found and nothing remains for us except to reproduce the same beliefs over and over. Religion is the fulfillment of life; it is an experience in which every aspect of being is raised to its highest state. What is needed to attain this, however, is not dogma, it is a change of consciousness, a rebirth, an inner revolution.

There is no such thing as the automatic evolution of man; this is possible only through his conscious effort. As he is, man remains an unfinished being. He must seek his own completion. He has to grow into a regenerate being and allow the Christ-consciousness to flow through him. This is the teaching of Christianity.

Jesus asks us to bring about this rebirth, but it can take place only through higher knowledge and meditation, not through external living habits or vocal prayer alone. When Jesus rebukes the Pharisees, for instance, he is condemning the man of pretenses who keeps up appearances. "Except your righteousness shall exceed the righteousness of the scribes and Pharisees," He said, "ye shall in no wise enter the Kingdom of Heaven." In other words, to attain heaven (which is the higher level of understanding) one has to grow, and this comes about through prayer, purity, self-control, studying life, and meditation. Christ and Buddha, for instance, freed themselves from the restricting notions of orthodox traditions, and that is the reason they could spread the Universal gospel of truth, love and service.

Jesus says of John the Baptist that he is the best of those born of women, but that the least of the kingdom of heaven was greater than he. For example, John speaks to us of salvation through moral life; he tells us what to do, but he does not tell us how to be. Jesus insists on inner transformation. John asks us to become better. Jesus asks us to become new. John the Baptist was puzzled when he heard that Jesus and His disciples ate and drank wine, and did not fast. He could not understand it when they plucked the ears of corn on the Sabbath day or when Jesus healed on the Sabbath. John is still a man born of woman; he has not experienced rebirth.

The writer of Ephesians says, "Except a man be born again he cannot see the Kingdom of God. Awake, thou that sleepest and arise from the dead." Originally, Christian teachings, before they became externalized and dogmatized, focused on awakening from sleep through the light shed by inner wisdom. Jesus Christ was one who had done this and who taught others the way.

Religion is not theology, and it is not magic or witchcraft. It should not spoil the simplicity of truth. Religion is not limited to the data of perception or introspection; it is experience to be lived, not a theory or belief to be accepted. When man surrounds his soul with a shell, such as national pride or the empty presumptions of dogma, he suppresses the breath of the spirit. Christianity, on the other hand, is a liberating power that is based on the life and experience of Jesus. The cross becomes significant when we make it our own and undergo crucifixion. Only then can we experience rebirth. "Seek and you shall find," said Jesus, but each of us must seek for himself. The truth that is latent in every soul must become manifest. Then shall we be able to work in newness of life.

"Marvel not that I have said unto thee, 'Ye must be born again'." In this spirit, says St. Paul, "your body is the temple of the Holy Ghost which is in you. . . . Know ye not that ye are the temple of God and that the spirit of God dwelleth in you? . . . You are the temple of the living God." He who enters inwardly, penetrates intimately into himself, and going beyond self, he becomes perfect.

In early Christianity meditation was practiced in all the monasteries and the cross, a symbol for physical suffering, mortification and earthly defeat, was also a symbol for spiritual victory. Through suffering lies the way of liberation.

Pascal says that Jesus struggles with death until the end of the world, and in this boundless Gethsemane which is the universe we have to struggle on unto death wherever a tear falls, wherever a heart is seized with despair, wherever an injustice or an act of violence is committed. "Hast thou seen thy brother, then thou hast seen God." This, the motto of the early Christians, is just as valid to us today.

Christianity's Witness to Meditation

Scriptural witness to meditation pervades both the Torah and the Gospels. For instance, in the Psalms one reads:

> Let the words of my mouth and the meditation of my heart be acceptable in thy sight, O lord my rock and my redeemer (Psalms 19:14).

> Be still and know that I am God (Psalms 46:10).

> I will hear that which God speaketh in me (Psalms 84:9 A.V. 85:8).

> I commune with my heart in the night; I meditate and search my spirit (Psalms 77:6).

> May my meditation be pleasing to him, for I rejoice in the Lord (Psalms 104:34).

> On the glorious splendor of thy majesty, and on thy wondrous works, I will meditate (Psalms 145:5).

Further witness of meditation in Christianity

can be found in the New Testament, which frequently shows Jesus retiring from the crowds to be alone in meditation, urging his followers to seek the "Father" within. Furthermore, in the Epistles St. Paul describes the whole unfolding of inner transformation as one progresses on the path to Christ-consciousness. These are but a few instances, among hundreds in the Bible, which clearly reflect the inner experiences of the higher nature. Somewhere, however, the thread between early and modern Christianity was broken, especially the tradition of initiation and meditation, and that is the reason why the modern Christian does not receive initiation in meditation. It is also one of the reasons why thousands of churches remain unattended on the day of worship. I do not mean that Western Christianity should accept Eastern beliefs *en toto*, but meditation is the means for developing the inner life, and this has been reaffirmed by the acknowledged mystics of Christianity. For example:

> Our meditation in this present life should be in the praise of God; for the external exultation of our life hereafter will be the praise of God: and none can become fit for the future life who hath not practiced himself for it now. (St. Augustine)

> Let me know myself, Lord, and I shall know Thee.
> (St. Augustine)

> No one can be saved without self-knowledge.
> (St. Bernard)

> Let us enter the cell of self-knowledge.
>
> (St. Catherine of Siena)

The above quotations, if deeply studied and properly understood, reveal that in the long line of Christian sages the practice of meditation was more essential than verbal prayer.

Many admirers of Christian mysticism may acknowledge the testimony of mystics but characterize these individuals as exceptional, their experiences beyond the potential of modern man. This pessimism endures because Western Christians are not aware of an overlooked tradition, one in which meditation was taught widely. This tradition at one time dominated early Christianity in the Middle East. For instance, after studying the history of the early Christians and the fathers of the desert, we know that they meditated day and night, and that meditation was not a new concept for them. Regardless of whether Abba, Paul or St. Anthony was the first monk and father of the desert, it is quite certain that St. Anthony established a school of very systematic meditation in 310 A.D. It was situated on a mountain called St. Anthony sixty-five miles south of Cairo, and there he guided thousands of monks on the path of meditation.

Another monastery, the monastery of Tabenna, in upper Egypt, was founded by Paul in 300 A.D. According to historical data, Paul was born a few years before the close of the third century, and later in his life he guided monks in practices similar to those of the school of St. Anthony. His school also endorsed the practice of silence.

In all, there were about five thousand monks practicing meditation and austerity in the Desert of Nitra, or the Nitron Valley, in Egypt, around that time, and during the second half of the fourth century a large number of ascetics lived all around Cairo. Christianity began to replace the myths and gods of Egypt, and the sign of the cross was often seen instead of the ancient symbols. The monastic life was so popular, as a matter of fact, that whole bodies of ascetics and mystics formed a veritable army in order to resist the government which opposed asceticism and mysticism—and this is one of the reasons why the secret methods of meditation could not be imparted to ordinary men in public.

To further trace the history of meditation in the West, it is mentioned in various scriptures that two monks from India accompanied Alexander the Great to the Middle East and established a school of meditation there. Meditation was a part of early Christian practices in the Middle East as well. History shows that early Christianity and Eastern Christianity had a long line of sages, competent in the art of meditation, and comparative studies reveal that their ascetic practices were very similar to, or the same as, those practiced by Indian monks and sages:

> The solitaries were very strict in the matter of food; they never took a full meal, seated comfortably at a table; flesh was never eaten; they believed in *ahimsa* (non-killing) and vegetarianism . . . . For fifteen years Ptolemy of the 'Klimas' in Nitria drank nothing but the dew he collected in sponges during the months of December and January each year.
>
> (Stories of the Holy Fathers)

> Patience and endurance were considered the greatest virtues; St. Anthony used to teach humility as the first and foremost principle for asceticism. There were numbers of women also practicing asceticism.
>
> (The Book of Paradise)

> And the blessed Anthony possessed this wonderful attribute. When he was dwelling in the mountain, his mind was alert and watchful to observe and to see, by the operation of the Holy Spirit which dwelt in him, that which was afar off as if it were near.
>
> (Stories of the Holy Fathers)

These words came from the deeper state of understanding, from the lips of men of meditation. There is no doubt in my mind that the fathers of the desert and of Mt. Athos, as well as St. Anthony, knew the methods of meditation, and this was the time when Patanjali's school of meditation was influencing the various sects and religions of the Far- and Middle East. Unfortunately, Western Christianity has never seriously absorbed this genuine meditative tradition.

It is also interesting to note that yogic breathing was practiced in the fifth century by the Hesychast monks. In addition, the spiritual writings of the Hesychastic period teach that the human body has certain focal points which correspond to the *chakras* of yoga—the navel, the heart, the throat and the mid-brow. The Hesychast monks, like the yogis, would concentrate upon these points in conjunction with rhythmic breathing and prayerful words, and by learning to control the respiration, the aspirant reached a tranquil state and tasted previously unknown spiritual experiences.

According to the Hesychasts (and to the yogis), as one progressed in the art of meditative breathing, the necessary ascetic practices gradually produced a transformation of character; disruptive feelings, ill thoughts and uncontrollable actions were gradually tranquilized by the steady practice of holy breathing (yogic breathing).

Later, during the Middle Ages, the confluence of Hesychastic prayer and meditation continued to prevail in Christian monasteries, and the great Byzantine mystic, St. Simeon, who lived from 949 to 1022 A.D., practiced and taught these methods of meditation *(Orientalia Christiana)*. One also finds the theory of breathing and the mystic physiology, called *sushumna dhyanam* in yogic manuals, in later, modern spiritual treatises (St. Teresa, St. John of the Cross), along with many references that relate breathing to various meditative states.

In addition, two orders who claim to have their own unbroken traditions—the Rosicrucians and Freemasonry—provide us with evidence to suggest a similar connection with yoga. (These two orders are very close and often work together). Freemasonry traces its antiquity to Solomon's Temple, and one finds in the esoteric and mystical history of both of these orders living testimonials to the fact that they used the symbol for what the yogis consider to be the mother sound, Om. For reference one can go through lectures on Masonic symbolism written by the late Grand Master Albert Pike who explains that Om was converted into Egyptian symbols:

> Coleman *(Mythology of the Hindus)* says that Om is a mystic symbol signifying the supreme God of Gods, which the Hindus, from its lawful and sacred meaning, hesitate to pronounce aloud, and in doing so place one of their hands before their mouths . . . .

Obstacles in the Path of Meditation

The practice of meditation in a systematic way, within a definite and accepted metaphysical framework, is congenial to all religious schools of the world, for their goal is the same—to bring the aspirants to the highest state of consciousness. Without having sufficient understanding of how and why meditation should be practiced, the meditative process can not lead to this highest state, but if the process is properly understood on all levels there will be inner peace and a unique experience of profound harmony along the way.

In attempting to achieve this meditative

experience, however, the aspirant is sooner or later threatened by two restrictions. The first is that the aspirant naturally tends to remain within the traditional boundaries of his accepted meta-physical and religious beliefs. This is his biggest obstacle. The second restriction is that the orthodox methods of meditation prescribed by Hindus, Buddhists, Jews or Christians discourage anyone from moving outside his own meditative approach.

Every theological system requires its followers to believe in a definite way, with definite notions of God, soul, heaven, hell, sin and virtue, but the pre-determined notions with which one goes to deeper states of meditation binds the meditator and prevents him from crossing the boundaries of his conditioned mind. One can receive higher experiences from this kind of meditation, but they are limited. Consequently, when one is restricted by dogma, one cannot realize the universal truth that the self within is the self of all. This enlightenment remains far away from the vision of the meditator.

Thus, to tread the path of enlightenment it is important for the meditator to fully understand a few terms which are often confusing:

Evil

For ages theologians have argued over the problem of evil. Why does it exist? Why is man not aware of truth? These questions have been answered by the rare and gifted ones who have transcended human consciousness (with its belief in good and evil).

Why do we dream? The answer can be found after we are awakened. Saints and sages who have attained Christ-consciousness, tell us that evil does not exist at all. (For those who are on the relative consciousness plane, the problem of how evil exists arises through academic and theological concepts.) We need only to know how to remove our ignorance, however, and we find that evil resides only in our sense of ego. Ego veils our eyes, and ignorance results. In reality, man is a spirit. He has a body, senses and mind, but when he forgets that he is a spirit and identifies himself with the body, senses and mind the sense of ego intervenes, and he forgets his superconscious nature. Thus, by living on the sense plane man becomes subject to believing in the devil, for with his consciousness fragmented by the attractions of the sense level, he fails to understand the incompatibility of affirming the existence of both God and the devil.

Ego

The problem of life amounts to this, whether one is a Hindu, Buddhist or Christian: how can one get rid of the ego? The answer given by the great sages of all religions is one and the same.

Surrender yourself to God, and love God with all your heart, mind and soul. Let individual consciousness be absorbed by God-consciousness. It sounds so simple—get rid of the ego, but it is the most difficult thing one can possibly do. If right discipline, patience and perseverance are practiced, it is possible. But the mind's tendencies towards the pleasant are usually stronger than its tendencies toward the good. The ego reasserts itself perpetually. Continuous sincere effort is the only way to get rid of it.

Belief

Often we console ourselves with the thought that God is sufficient for enlightenment, but unless there is a clear conception of what this means, there cannot be unfoldment. Distorted beliefs halt growth. Knowledge alone dispels the darkness of ignorance. Believing in God is a positive help, but enlightenment is not possible without direct experience. No freedom is possible by mere belief. For instance, just as the experiences in a dream which resembles life make us happy or unhappy, so do we obtain freedom when we awaken and know the reality, which is direct knowledge. In order to gain this freedom, however, one must have an earnest desire to attain higher knowledge.

A one-pointed mind is essential to God-realization, but we should approach truth through one way only. If one practices meditation in one way today and another tomorrow, for instance, it does not make the mind one-pointed. (It is really amazing that teachers give their students many different objects to meditate upon, for this does not help the mind to become steady.) Unless there is only one chosen ideal (or object to love or meditate upon), there cannot be any progress.

Single-minded devotion towards one's ideal is also very important. Suppose the ideal is Christ. You should know that this same ideal is meditated upon by others in various names and forms, and you should know that this same ideal is the absolute unmanifested One. The Christ is your soul, and you should learn to see Him in all beings, to feel and know that He is your shepherd and treasure. You should awaken the faculty of spiritual discrimination, to know the difference between the real and the unreal, and you will know that Christ is the abiding reality; all else is merely appearance. With such knowledge, liberation is possible, but it should be combined with earnest desire, sincere effort and spiritual discipline. Otherwise, progress is impossible.

Prayer and Meditation

Prayer is communication between the lower and higher domains; and it often takes the shape of a petition. Meditation, on the other hand, is a continuation of one thought. Here, individual interests are transcended by a one-pointed mind which desires to fathom the desireless and un-fathomable realms of life. There is a further difference between petitionary prayer, contemplation and meditation. In petitionary prayer there is always a demand for something. In contemplation one contemplates (ponders) certain ideals. In meditation one transcends the thinking process and all conditioning of the mind. In prayer and contemplation there is an awareness of duality, but in meditation, when the final state has been reached there is a "yoking" of the soul with God, directly. All the metaphysical and religious laws are left behind when one reaches the highest state of experience and unity. True, there are various types of invocations –silent prayers, concentration and contemplation—but only meditation expands individual consciousness to universal Christ-consciousness.

The Unfoldment of Meditation

The word *meditation* is used in various ways, but it always applies to techniques which deal with man's inner nature. Through these techniques one finally transcends all levels of the mind and goes on to Christ-consciousness and realization of the absolute one. Meditation does not require a belief in dogma or in any authority. It is an inward journey in which one studies one's own self on all levels, finally going to the source of consciousness. The aim of meditation is Self-realization; it is a direct vision of truth. It is not an intellectual pursuit, nor is it emotional rapture. The whole being is involved. It is neither suppression (which makes one passive), nor is it a gaining of any experience which is not already within us.

Meditation leads one from want to wantlessness. It is a way of going from the known to the unknown. The process can hardly be explained by words, but it leads one from the personal, through the transpersonal, finally uniting him with the highest one. It transforms the whole personality.

Life is a series of experiences, but all experiences do not lead us and become guides in the path of unfoldment. There are experiences, however, which great sages have witnessed from the deeper realms of their being, experiences which are not considered to come from the contact of the senses or sense objects. The sages talk of the bliss proceeding from the inner depths of the self, the eternal spring of bliss that lies within the heart of man; its realization is life-fulfillment and wisdom. Like the kingdom of heaven in the parable of Jesus, it is found not in some place remote from life, but within life itself:

> And when he was demanded of the Pharisees, when the kingdom of God should come, he answered them and said, 'The kingdom of God cometh not with observation. Neither shall they say, Lo, here! or, Lo, there! for, behold, the kingdom of God is within you.' (Luke 17:20-21).

By what means can such an experience be obtained? Most often Western Christians condemn the philosophy of meditation (which is actually the heart of Christianity), but yoking with God, or Christ-consciousness, cannot be realized by merely reciting the verses of the Bible and sayings of Christ.

> Man if thou wishest to know what it is to pray ceaselessly: Enter into thyself, and interrogate the Spirit of God.
>
> Angelus Silesius (Cherub 1:237)

Jesus expresses this truth in the New Testament:

> Ask, and it shall be given unto you; seek and ye shall find; knock, and it shall be opened unto you. For every one that asketh, receiveth; and he that seeketh, findeth; and to him that knocketh, it shall be opened.
>
> (Matt. 7:7-8)

> And when thou prayest, thou shalt not be as the hypocrites are: for they love to pray standing in the synagogues and in the corners of the streets, that they may be seen of men. Verily I say unto you, they have their reward. But thou, when thou prayest, enter into thy closet, and when thou has shut thy door, pray to thy Father which is in secret; and thy Father which seeth in secret shall reward thee openly.
>
> (Matt. 6:5-6)

"Seek and ye shall find." But how do we realize this truth? When man forgets his true nature, that "Kingdom of God within," he loses his way in the tangle of the world. Who will show him the way back to what he has forgotten? Only he himself can do this. The purer the mind, the more easily it is controlled and disciplined, and a pure, disciplined mind finds its way to God.

The whole process of spiritual and ethical discipline leads man to the awareness of the reality existing behind man and nature. Through the senses man becomes aware of differences, but through Christ-consciousness he becomes aware of the unity that is behind these differences. Just as ethics discovers laws which link the different aspects of sense experience, the philosophy of meditation unravels the laws of yoking man with the ultimate one.

Meditation is a search within oneself on various levels, finally leading to that center from whence consciousness flows. A proper method of meditation helps one in discovering the ultimate unifying principle of the universe, and when properly-understood and rightly-practiced methods for spiritual growth are applied, they will guide one toward the only way of transcending the self and going to the superconscious state.

In other words, when a man is moved by the deeper problems and starts questioning himself, mere promises in the scriptures do not satisfy him. When a man realizes the importance of life and its purpose, then he turns to the philosophy of meditation and finds the solutions therein. Patanjali, for instance, in the *Yoga Sutras*, outlines a systematic and detailed training program, free of religious bias, for anyone who wants to learn meditation, and the millions of people in both the East and the West who are genuinely interested in meditation can follow his guidelines regardless of their religion.

From the very beginning, meditation requires a seeking and a logical mind, a questioning mind, aided by the help of the right method. In addition, the seeker must perform his actions selflessly, with love, one-pointedness, self-purity and righteousness. Otherwise, the yoking of the mind is not possible.

Thus, meditation, in its creative and dynamic aspects, can be practiced, first, by having the right spiritual attitude—by performing selfless action in the external world. This is called meditation in action (Bhagavad Gita). Another method of meditation is to sit in a calm and quiet place, on a firm seat, in a relaxed and comfortable posture. Then become aware of the breath, and then make the mind one-pointed by allowing the mind to attend to the flow of breath. When the mind has become concentrated, the word or *mantra* (a sound or word to make the mind one-pointed) given for meditation should be remembered. Constant remembrance of the *mantra* leads the student to a higher state of mind, and such a mind is capable of going beyond its limitations. Finally, when the mind goes out of the dimensions of its own created conditions, there dawns Christ-consciousness.

This second type of meditation has been practiced by yogis and monks who have devoted their
whole lives to realizing the truth. First, they
withdraw their sense awareness from the objects
of the world and their physical selves; second,
they concentrate their minds on a *mantra*. Then,
when the mind starts flowing like a stream of oil,
it becomes one-pointed and can transcend the
limitations of emotional and rational boundaries.
Thus, new habits are formed and old habits are
cast off. This is called spiritual rebirth.

In other words, when the mind constantly
thinks of God meditation becomes a constant
remembrance, and it flows like an unbroken
stream. In such a case there cannot be any bondage; constant recollection and ceaseless prayer
become a means to liberation, and meditation
becomes constant remembering. So in order to
have an unbroken memory of God, one should
meditate regularly. It should be an unceasing
flow toward God within. Then, when one constantly lives, moves and has his being in God, the
body becomes a temple.

Theology says that God exists and we should
believe in Him. Philosophy says, Know the relationship of man, the universe, and its Creator.
Meditation gives a direct vision of God in the temple of the body. A man of meditation does not
have to search, roam and wander in pursuit of
God; he finds his beloved within himself. The
foolish man keeps searching on the sense plane

(for all the distractions are at the outer gate of the temple), but when one enters into the inner chamber, shutting the outer gate, he finds his majesty, the center of Christ-consciousness. He is reborn and becomes a free citizen of the kingdom of God. Such a man becomes universal.

For instance, the practice of love is the natural awareness of God, and those who are constantly aware of the reality of the Lord within become the beloved of the Lord. They alone gain liberation; they receive direction and can guide others.

Thus, to be perfect and to attain the kingdom of heaven is the attainable goal of man. It is within us all. Man stands midway between the visible and invisible worlds—but to get at the inner experience we must abstract from the outer. That is what Erasmus meant when he delivered the great dictum, "Wherever you encounter truth, look upon it as Christianity."

It should be remembered that all great religions teach fundamentally this same truth, but that the great messengers of this truth tear down traditional values and establish a new order, according to the need of their times. By transcending national, religious and traditional boundaries, meditation transforms an individual into a cosmic man. The result of meditation is therefore revolution, for it brings about a transformation of the personality of the meditator. False values are left behind and new values are established. Thus starts reformation in the world.

Meditation in the Bible

Reverend Lawrence Bouldin

The essence of religion is to awaken us to a full awareness of that great center of peace, wisdom and freedom which lies veiled in the self within us. "Seek first the kingdom of God," taught the master, Jesus, stressing that one's primary duty in life is to seek an unfolding consciousness of our unity with God within and without. The purpose of the scriptures is to assist in this, the basic mission of human life, by continually directing those who aspire to eternal truth to seek ever higher levels of spiritual awareness.

Scriptures are read and studied by those who are at quite different stages in their development of spiritual awareness, and what can be understood by some remains shrouded in darkness for others. What is a key to advancement for one may be read with little appreciation by another. Still, it is a basic tenet of the ancient tradition that the deeper levels of meaning in the scriptures will be revealed to persons who are ready to understand them, and to his inner circle of disciples Jesus revealed the hidden meaning of his teachings: "To you has been given the secret of the kingdom of God, but for those outside everything is in parables" (Mk. 4:11).

Scriptures are written with the understanding that what is appropriate for feeding to infants will no longer satisfy mature persons. The corollary is also true that no sensible mother would even try to feed her babe with the same whole food she gives her husband. So, too, in spiritual growth, what is given to spiritual babes is carefully prepared to nourish them in infancy, and when they mature they will receive food of another kind. "Every one who lives on milk is unskilled in the word of righteousness, for he is a child. But solid food is for the mature, for those who have their faculties trained by practice . . ." (Heb. 4:13,14).

In the early church those who studied the scriptures knew that the writings contained various strata of meaning. Today this approach is largely neglected. Each sect reads to find textual support for its own doctrinal statements, and dogma has supplanted the scriptures as the basis of teaching. Even theologians and biblical scholars, while engaged in the "search for the historical Jesus," have overlooked the central concern of the scriptures which is to reveal the "universal Christ."

Jesus always pointed to the deeper meanings of his words by saying, "He who has ears to hear, let him hear," which is to say that a purified mind will comprehend the true significance of his teachings. At the same time, he warned his disciples not to cast their pearls before swine, not to spend truth foolishly on those who are unwilling to heed it, nor to reveal esoteric wisdom to those who are morally and intellectually unprepared to receive it.

The power generated by truth is turned to destructive ends in the hands of those whose motivations flow from selfish desires. But to those of purified heart and mind, truth was given to draw them more fully into the consciousness of the divine plan. Paul wrote: "We impart a secret and hidden wisdom of God, which God decreed before the ages for our glorification . . . . As it is written, 'What no eye has seen, nor ear heard, nor the heart of man conceived, what God has prepared for those who love Him,' God has revealed to us through the Spirit. For the Spirit searches everything, even the depths of God. For what person knows a man's thoughts except the Spirit of the man which is in him? So also no one comprehends the thoughts of God except the Spirit of God. Now we have received not the spirit of the world, but the Spirit which is from God, that we might understand the gifts bestowed on us by God" (1 Cor. 2:7-12).

The highest spiritual knowledge reflected in the Bible is not the result of sense perceptions, as is much of our normal knowledge of the world. Nor, says Paul, is deep spiritual awareness the result of thinking with the mind, as are many of the ideas we produce each day. Instead, spiritual truth is revealed to those who become aware, through meditation, of the presence of God's spirit within us. It is in this state that all is known, "even the depths of God." In this way Paul teaches that through meditation alone (the state which is beyond sense perception and thinking) does one experience the reality of eternal truth and absolute being through the awareness of God's spirit within the inner chamber of the self.

Origen, the great Christian scholar of the third century, applied to the Bible a three-level method of interpretation commonly used by the sages of ancient Eastern thought. According to this, scriptures have a "body," which is the external, factual, historical content that has been recorded. Above that foundation, scriptures have a "soul," which is the ethical meaning of the event as it is applied to the character or experience of their students. And, highest of all, there is the "spirit" of the scriptures, or the esoteric, allegorical meaning known only to those who have "the mind of Christ." To these qualified persons has been revealed (while they were in a state of super-conscious meditation) the essential unity of the individual with God, the ultimate experience of human life toward which the scriptures are intended to lead us. (Origen, *De Principis*, Preface, Book IV.)

The Bible presents meditation as the technique by which persons may enter into full awareness of the "spirit" of the scriptures, into the experience of truth and essential being. Jesus, whose anointing as Christ signaled His own self-realization, declared: "I am the Way, the Truth and the Life; no one comes to the Father but by Me." (Jn. 14:6). Christ-consciousness, achieved through meditation by sincere aspirants, then, is the direct experience of God as truth and truth as God. It is the way which reveals that the seeker, the path and the goal are ultimately one. To come to the Father by way of Christ-consciousness is the only way in which one can attain to the state of union. The freedom which comes with the knowledge of the truth (Jn. 8:32) is the experience expressed in the Master's words, "I and My Father are one" (Jn. 10:30).

Meditation can be practiced by any sincere and disciplined disciple: "Let him who is thirsty, let him who desires take the waters of life without price" (Rev. 22:17b). Those who hunger and thirst after righteousness are promised satisfaction (Matt. 5:6).

The prophet Isaiah spoke of the meditative path as the way of holiness. In the passage that follows, the holy way is meditation, but it is clearly stated that it is a way open only to those of purified heart. (Jesus later was to say that only the pure of heart would see God.) The passage also describes the result of meditation: freedom from fear and its consequent destruction, deliverance from the threat of danger which springs from the sense of separateness and alienation in

the external world, the realization of unity with
God and the experience of everlasting joy, bliss
and peace.

> And a highway shall be there,
> And it shall be called the Holy Way;
> The unclean shall not pass over it,
> And fools shall not err therein.
> No lion shall be there,
> Nor shall any ravenous beast come up on it;
> They shall not be found there,
> But the redeemed shall walk there.
> And the ransomed of the Lord shall return,
> And come to Zion with singing,
> With everlasting joy upon their heads;
> They shall obtain joy and gladness,
> And sorrow and sighing shall flee away.
>   (Isaiah 35:8-10)

Here, Zion is a symbol for the state of exalted
consciousness attained through meditation.

In the Book of Psalms there are repeated
references to meditation; the word "meditation,"
in fact, appears here more often than in any
other book of the Bible, and one of the most
beautiful songs about meditation is Psalm 91. It
begins with the verse:

> He who dwells in the shelter of the Most High,
> Who abides in the shadow of the Almighty,
> Will say to the Lord, "My refuge and my fortress;
> My God, in whom I trust."

Speaking thus of the meditative state as the "sha-
dow of the Almighty," the psalmist goes on to

describe the security, tranquility, joy and attainment of the one who meditates. The almighty one blesses the individual who approaches Him through meditation with the promise of deliverance, saying, "I will . . . show him My salvation."

The way of meditation is the path to which seekers for God are ultimately drawn. In Psalm 1 the righteous person is described as one who meditates on God's law by day and by night, asserting that his roots are securely planted beside the stream of life. "In all that he does, he prospers" (Ps. 1:6) for he is one with the fountainhead of prosperity.

Throughout the Bible there are numerous traditional symbols which represent the state of meditation and which give further insight into the depth of God-consciousness experienced by the sages of the Judeo-Christian heritage. For instance, one of the repeated symbols for meditation is "silence." This state is praised in many of the Psalms, for it is only when one enters the silence beyond senses and thinking that one is directly aware of the presence of the Lord within: "Be still, and know that I am God" (Ps. 46:10). The seeker of eternal wisdom enters the meditative state for one purpose only—to be merged into the universal consciousness of the absolute: "For God alone my soul waits in silence" (Ps. 62:1).

Job, the sage afflicted by every sort of trial, clearly depicts the battle that every aspirant must wage against the domination of the senses, desires, and the tyranny of mind. Finally stripped of every material, emotional and mental attachment, Job is ready to heed the voice of the silence that leads to enlightenment, "Be silent, and I will teach you wisdom" (Job 33:33).

In the Book of Revelation, an esoteric Christian guide to meditation, we find a reference to the passage of time while in a superconscious state: " . . . there was silence in heaven for about half an hour" (Rev. 8:1). Here the reference to "heaven" is also a symbol for meditation leading to superconscious awareness. And Jesus, in one of His clearest statements about meditation, directed His disciples to cultivate the habit of seeking regularly the silent inner chamber: "When you pray, go into your room and shut the door and pray to your Father who is in secret" (Matt. 6:6).

Another favorite biblical symbol of the state of superconscious meditation is "light," and Jesus spoke of Christ-consciousness as the light of perfect discrimination by which persons will know the real from the unreal: "I am the light of the world; he who follows Me will not walk in darkness, but will have the light of life" (Jn. 8:12). Light is also one of the most extensive symbols for ancient wisdom, having cosmic significance as well as being a symbol for spiritual enlightenment. It encompasses the creative power embodied in the self-manifestation of the absolute as well as the ultimate achievement of human life. The cosmic dimension of spiritual unfoldment is indicated in Paul's statement, "It is the God who said, 'Let light shine out of darkness,' who has shone in our hearts to give the light of the knowledge of the glory of God in the face of Christ" (2 Cor. 4:6).

As giver of light in the universe, the sun symbolizes the highest state of superconscious meditation. Once attained, the enlightened state does not disappear, for the consciousness of the individual remains focused "there" even in the midst of activity "here." The rising of the sun of enlightenment signifies the soul's final liberation from the bonds of the world:

Your sun shall no more go down,
Nor your moon withdraw itself;
For the Lord will be your
Everlasting light,
And your days of mourning
Shall be ended.
(Is. 60:20)

Still another favorite biblical symbol for meditation is seen in the many references to the "temple." Throughout the whole Judeo-Christian tradition the temple is that place to which man goes to worship the Lord who dwells in the innermost chamber, the "Holy of Holies." The real significance of the temple, however, is not the physical building, or place of worship, but the temple within each person. "The God who made the world and everything in it, being Lord of heaven and earth, does not live in shrines made by man, nor is he served by human hands, as though he needed anything, since he himself gives to all men life and breath and everything . . . . He is not far from each one of us, for 'In him we live and move and have our being' " (Acts 17:24-28).

God is spirit and must be worshipped in the temple of spirit, in meditative union with Him. It is this innermost temple to which the prophet made reference when he said, "The Lord is in his holy temple: let all the earth keep silence before him (Hab. 2:20). Paul also wrote of this inner presence of God, "Do you not know that you are God's temple and that God's Spirit dwells in you? . . . For God's temple is holy, and that temple you are" (1 Cor. 3:16, 17). Meditation begins when a person ceases looking for ultimate reality in that which is external to himself and becomes aware of the presence of God within. To go beyond oneself in search of God means to turn inwards to the core of life which is the essence of God's own being.

The greatest biblical insight related to the symbol of God's temple is found in the story of the boy Jesus' visit to the temple with his parents. As told in Luke 2:41-51, Jesus accompanies his parents to Jerusalem for the feast of the Passover. When his parents return home, Jesus remains in the temple. After three days they find him sitting in the temple among the teachers, and in response to their anxiety about his failure to return home with them, Jesus answers, "How is it that you sought me? Did you not know that I must be in my Father's house?"

Here the temple symbolizes the meditative state in which man experiences his essential unity with God. It is to this temple that we make our way again and again in search of joy, peace, wisdom and real prosperity of spirit. The return of Mary and Joseph to their home represents our turning to the cares and life of the world (where renewed confusion is the inevitable result). With the attainment of self-realization, however, the consciousness of Christ remains focused in the temple, the Father's house. And even when attention is partially redirected to the world (Jesus did go home again with his parents), from that time on the individual consciousness remains essentially united with the universal consciousness of Christ. We learn through this story that enlightenment requires a universalization of consciousness, that the "sanctuary frame of mind" must be entered into and maintained throughout the whole day.

Additional symbols for the meditative state abound in the Bible. A few more should be mentioned briefly before passing on to a consideration of the necessity for meditation in the life of the aspirant. The state of meditation is sometimes symbolized by a dream, a vision, or a voice speaking as from God. The great prophet Elijah failed to discern God in external phenomena, but became aware of the divine presence as "a still small voice" within (1 Kgs. 19:12). Isaiah wrote of a similar experience: "Your ears shall hear a word behind you, saying, 'This is the way, walk in it. '" (Is. 30:21).

Mountains and other high places represent the lifting of consciousness above the mundane levels of sense and thinking. Throughout the whole chronicle of salvation history in the Old and New Testaments, the great events took place on a mountain or hill: Moses received the Ten Commandments in an exalted state of consciousness (on a hill); the Sermon on the Mount of Jesus epitomizes New Testament spiritual awareness; the spiritual Transfiguration of Christ was set on a mountain. The word of the Lord comes time and again to His devout ones: "Go forth, and stand upon the mount before the Lord" (1 Kgs. 19:11). If God is to be perceived, if man is to unfold in universal consciousness, his awareness must be lifted above the "here" of sense and thought to the "there" of meditative union with the Father.

The sounding of the trumpet is another symbol for meditation and the state of superconsciousness. Jeremiah admonished his people: "Give heed to the sound of the trumpet" (Jer. 6:17). The trumpet call is one of the keys to the transition from one stage of meditation to another in the book of Revelation of John.

The head (sometimes depicted in art with a halo), altars, the ark of the covenant, anointment with oil, wellsprings and many more symbols are additional means for conveying the deep allegorical truths about the meditative path to holiness.

Not only does the Bible contain such extensive symbolic reference to meditation as has been briefly surveyed. The Bible also offers to the serious student a deeper understanding of the importance—the necessity—of meditating.

As Jesus began his public teaching he announced the nature of his mission—liberation. From the book of the prophet Isaiah he read:

> The Spirit of the Lord is upon me,
> Because he has anointed me to preach good news
>   to the poor,
> He has sent me to proclaim release to the captives
> And recovery of sight to the blind,
> To set at liberty those who are oppressed,
> To proclaim the acceptable year of the Lord.

Then Jesus said, "Today this scripture has been fulfilled in your hearing" (Lk. 4:18-21).

Jesus taught what he experienced himself: that liberation from the bonds of suffering and death comes only with the attainment of the state of Christ-consciousness. What was possible for the master, Jesus, is possible to those who follow His way: " . . . where I am you may be also" (Jn. 14:3).

Jesus emphasized the contrast between bondage and eternal freedom by using images of death and life. He said, "I came that they might have life" (Jn. 10:10), meaning that through meditation one may achieve liberation from that which binds him back to the level of life (which is characterized by suffering and death). The paradox of "living though dying" exemplifies the truth of awakening to eternal unity with God through the consciousness of the indwelling Christ: "I am the resurrection and the life; he who believes in me, though he die, yet shall he live, and whosoever lives and believes in me shall never die" (Jn. 11:25, 26).

With the awakening of the individual to the reality of a spiritual realm of eternal dimensions, all of one's experience begins to fall into proper perspective. What once seemed important is no longer attractive, for it is seen to be temporal and unsatisfying. There is a growing realization that before one can be a possessor of the eternal fruits of the spirit, he must rid himself of the attachments which bind him to earth. The *karmic* ties of desire which manifest in the passions must be overcome by redirecting all of our urges toward the one goal of liberation into unity with God. As Jesus said to his followers: "Where your treasure is, there shall your heart be also" (Lk. 12:34).

If a person's heart is attached to the objects, seen and unseen, of the physical and mental planes, he is locked into the cycle of temporality. When, however, his vision is lifted to the plane of spirit he is freed for eternity. "The things which are seen are temporal," wrote Paul, "but the things which are not seen are eternal" (2 Cor. 4:13).

Meditation is a necessary part of the aspirant's discipline because it is the only means available by which he can be freed from the lower attachments and begin to focus in the spiritual realm.

This shift in attention from the plane of sense perceptions to the realm of the spirit is identified in the Bible as the humanizing event, the "coming of age" of man through the realization of his human potential. In the Old Testament there are numerous references similar to this one from Ezekiel: "A new heart I will give you, and a new spirit I will put within you; and I will take out of your flesh the heart of stone and give you a heart of flesh. And I will put my spirit within you . . . ." (Ezek. 36:26,17). Henceforward, those who have received this spirit may attain the stature of full human dignity which is the measure of the fulness of Christ (Eph. 4:13).

In the Bible the crowning achievement of man is to attain to the level of Christ-consciousness. This is the significance of the invitation of Jesus, "Follow me." This attainment of Christ-consciousness is portrayed in a verse from the last book of the Bible: "Then I looked, and lo, a white cloud, and seated on the cloud one like the son of man, with a golden crown on his head, and a sharp sickle in his hand" (Rev. 14:14). In this image the cloud represents the state of meditation, and the son of man is universalized, or Christ-consciousness attained through meditation. The golden crown directs our attention to the implicit claim that this state is the loftiest achievement of human life. And finally, the sickle is the faculty of discrimination sharpened by meditation, without which the spiritual harvest could not be reaped. Discrimination of the real from the unreal, the light from darkenss and immortality from mortality is that which leads to liberation from the bonds of temporality.

Christ-consciousness is not reached without constant effort on the part of the seeker, nor is the path of spiritual unfoldment an easy one to walk. Matthew records these words of Jesus: "Enter by the narrow gate; for the gate is wide and the way is easy, that leads to destruction, and those who enter by it are many. For the gate is narrow and the way is hard, that leads to life, and those who find it are few" (Matt. 7:13.14). As an explicit statement that to achieve deep meditation requires firm spiritual discipline and as an observation that many will fail to bring themselves to this level of realization, these words of Jesus parallel the words of Krishna in the *Bhagavad Gita:* "Out of many thousands among men, one may endeavor for perfection, and of those who have attained perfection, hardly one knows Me in truth" (7:3).

Difficult though it may be from the relative perspective of man, spiritual attainment is the culminating experience towards which all human life is striving. When men have finally exhausted their many desires for pleasures and powers, they become aware of the inner call to realize that which is eternal within themselves. When man is ready, he finds God waiting to reveal Himself both as the goal and as the path. "Behold, I stand at the door and knock; if any one hears My voice and opens the door, I will come into him and eat with him and he with Me" (Rev. 3:20).

Jesus emphasized in his teaching that though the way appears difficult, to him who surrenders himself to the Lord the path of spiritual seeking is like looking for the path that leads home (the parable of the Prodigal Son). He taught that for those who are ready, the way will become clear. Progress becomes natural and even easy for those who are fully committed to the goal: "Come to Me, all who labor and are heavy laden, and I will give you rest. Take My yoke upon you, and learn from Me; for I am gentle and lowly in heart, and you will find rest for your souls. For My yoke is easy, and my burden is light" (Matt. 12:28-30). The word *yoke* is from the same Sanskrit root as the word *yoga*; both signify union, or binding together, and are used in appropriate contexts to indicate the preliminary disciplines as well as the achieved state of God-realization, or universal Christ-consciousness, which is the goal of all spiritual effort.

It is this striving, represented by the discipline of the yoke, that brings the seeker to the eventual realization of God. "I and the Father are one" (Jn. 10:30), said the Christ. To enter into this consciousness is to become merged with God in a conscious way, for " . . . where I am you may be also" (Jn. 14:3).

The Christ declared his continuous presence among his disciples; "Lo, I am with you always, to the close of the age" (Matt. 28:20). By this he meant that Self-realization (the realization of God within) is an ever-present possibility because it is an ever-present reality, though in a latent state of awareness. The power, awakened in the aspirant, to achieve this level of superconscious awareness is the power of the indwelling Christ in every person. Jesus used the parable of the vine and branches to teach his followers that they have life only in God, not through any power of their own. We live in God; God lives in us. Our spiritual power is the power of God manifesting in us. When we become aware of our true nature we realize that "apart from me you can do nothing" (Jn. 15:5). At the same time the realization, through meditation, of our true nature shows us the unimagined heights we can attain. Jesus quoted the scriptures saying, "you are gods" as evidence for the claim that "the Father is in me and I am in the Father" (Jn. 10:34,38). Knowing this, we are guided into the great truth, "the Spirit of truth whom the world cannot receive" (Jn. 14:17), the truth of which Christ said, "You shall know the truth, and the truth shall make you free" (Jn. 8:32). The great truth of life is our essential and eternal unity with God, which truth, when it is experienced, frees us from all bondage of suffering and ignorance. Knowing this, a man knows all he needs to know, for he has become one with the eternal: "I, when I am lifted up from the earth, will draw all men to Myself" (Jn. 12:32).

To realize Christ in oneself, then, is the goal of the Christian's spiritual discipline. Symbolically, the seeker must die to the self of his lower nature and be born again in the higher consciousness of Christ within. Through meditation he becomes focused in the new dimension: "I have been crucified with Christ; it is no longer I who live, but Christ who lives in me" (Gal. 2:20).

Crucifixion and resurrection are a part of the Christian way to the realization of God. The old self of the lower nature is put to death; the new self of Christ-consciousness is raised to eternal life. Awareness of body, senses, emotions and thoughts are withdrawn into the cave of death; the candle of realization shines brightly in the inner chamber of the self. The individual self dies; Christ lives within. By following this path of crucifixion and resurrection through meditation, the individual attains the goal:

> Whatever gain I had, I counted as loss for the sake of Christ. Indeed I count everything as loss because of the surpassing worth of knowing Christ . . . that I may know Him and the power of His resurrection.
> (Phil. 3:7-10).

In the book of the Revelation of John, this attainment is called the "crown of life" (Rev. 2: 10), symbolizing achievement of the highest goal in life and the price of eternity through union with God. Jesus taught the surpassing value of Self-realization through inner awareness of the Father and told his disciples that they could expect to know only prolonged death and suffering so long as they sought to save their lives through attachment to physical and mental securities. "For whoever would save his life will lose it, and whoever loses his life for my sake will find it. For what will it profit a man if he gains the whole world and forfeits his life?" (Matt. 16:25).

To reach the end for which meditation is the means is to experience the bliss, wisdom and peace of God. Jesus spoke of this peace as his great gift to his followers: "Peace I leave with you; my peace I give to you" (Jn. 14:27). In the peace of God is the steadiness of knowing that there will never be separation from the Father. This great affirmation of life is summarized by Paul in his letter to the Romans:

> For I am sure that neither death, nor life, nor angels, nor principalities, nor things present, nor things to come, nor powers, nor height, nor depth, nor anything in all creation, will be able to separate us from the love of God in Christ Jesus our Lord (Rom. 8:38,39).

The story of Stephen provides an appropriate

conclusion to this account of the place of meditation in the Bible. As told in the Acts of the Apostles, his story is a revelation of that glorious experience which comes to a God-enlightened man who knows that nothing can destroy his essential union with God. He is described as a man "full of the Spirit and of wisdom" (6:3) whose face "was like the face of an angel" (6:15) in the hour of his realization. The culmination of his unfoldment into full awareness of God came in the form of a vision:

> He, full of the Holy Spirit, gazed into heaven and saw the glory of God, and Jesus standing at the right hand of God; and he said, "Behold I see the heavens opened, and the Son of man standing at the right hand of God."
>
> (Acts 7:55, 56)

The Bible is filled with these and many more references to meditation and the attainment of God-realization. There is no other goal worthy of our commitment, and, as we have seen, the Christ of the Bible is both the power and the symbol of that high attainment to which we are called.

Meditation in the
Book of Revelation

Justin O'Brien, Ph.D.

For the ordinary reader of the Bible, the Apocalypse, or Revelation of St. John, is an enigma, a puzzling departure from the clarity and detail which characterizes the balance of the New Testament. Contrasted with the gospel writings, for instance, the Book of Revelation reveals no more of the circumstances under which it was written than a few statements regarding John's exile on Patmos island and his intention to write to certain Christian communities in Asia Minor. Aside from this meager bit of information, the structure and content of the book seem to be a labyrinth of esoteric symbolism for even the most astute of readers. Modern biblical scholars frequently admit that the complexities of language in John's prophetic vision exceed their best exegetical skills, and even with the fresh insights of current anthropology, archaeology and philology, Revelation remains veiled.

While this may not be cause for alarm to the churches (since they have survived for centuries already without fathoming the esoteric truths of Revelation) still there lingers in our minds the hope that this exceptional book will yield much to help the genuine seeker for God.

Reason and faith alike have been insufficient as expository tools for opening the Apocalypse to our understanding. All we can be sure about is that John was meditating one day and had an extraordinary vision which he evokes for his readers. As unexpected as it may sound, the clue to deciphering Revelation may be just as simple as remembering that he is describing a meditative experience. The whole context of Revelation, in fact, assures us that the author was not presenting a speculative tract on theological topics. Instead, the writing reflects a series of interior experiences of a highly symbolic character. What is more, John starts by telling us what he is doing—meditating—thereby signaling his readers to approach the text in a different way from that of traditional exegesis.

The churches insist that Revelation is divinely inspired, that it belongs officially to the canon and thus deserves faithful study, but they do not provide the key to the hidden significance of the writing. This is of no help to one who seeks ultimate truths. In other words, the traditional acceptance of its place in the scriptures does not relieve the serious student of the task of seeking to unravel the mysteries of the book's elaborate symbolism.

Current biblical criticism has proven unsuccessful in uncovering the real significance of Revelation because its research employs only discursive analysis; the prolonged inability of conventional exegetical methods to illuminate Revelation is virtually assured by the continuing failure to examine the state of consciousness indicated by the author. To move beyond this impasse two guidelines are proposed: first, the process of gradual interiorization, known as nondiscursive meditation, serves as a point of practical departure for the reader and simultaneously provides him with the interpretive key for unlocking the Apocalypse; second, the profound disclosures in John's meditation may be compared profitably with ancient Eastern writings which elucidate the particular state of consciousness which gives rise to them. The latter proposal should not seem out of place when we consider the geographical and cultural situation of the author.

Among the Upanishads (texts of Eastern culture) there are Sanskrit writings which describe in detail the states of consciousness that St. John passed through. These reflect definite steps, or levels of consciousness, which come about by means of the meditative process. In comparing John's experiences with this tradition, then, we are not inferring that an hallucinatory, or purely subjective, condition prevailed in him. On the contrary, his personal experiences take on a universal significance when the reader can understand the physical and mental modifications involved in achieving this remarkable state of awareness. Through the insights provided by

Eastern texts, then, the Book of Revelation takes on dimension it did not gain from conventional exegesis.

Just as the final goal of Christians is face-to-face knowledge of God, so also do those who follow the Eastern paths to God strive for a similar achievement which they refer to as "conscious union," or yoga. The latter is a Sanskrit term which indicates the path to achievement, and tantric yoga, one of several branches of yoga science, teaches that the normal human body has available an unusual power source residing near the base of the spine. Through the release of this power, the human body and consciousness undergo radical changes in their composition and level of awareness, respectively.

In Sanskrit symbolism this *kundalini shakti*, or creative force, is visualized as a sleeping serpent coiled at the base of the spine with its mouth covering the actual base. Its power is dormant because of an intoxicating nectar seeping into its mouth through the vertical column known as the *sushumna* (comparable to the spinal column). The task of the meditator is to awaken and sustain the rising power, or searching serpent.

When the dripping nectar ceases flowing (having been halted deliberately by the aspiring yogi) the serpent awakens and travels upward in search of the missing elixir, and the *sushumna*, or pathway of upward travel, leads the serpent through a series of seven *chakras*, or centers of consciousness.

In the makeup of the human individual these *chakras* are generally associated with the centers located along the length of the spine. Through these centers the endocrine system and the connecting plexuses serve as the physical agencies which manifest the activity of the *chakras* which are not, however, to be identified with their physical counterparts. The word *chakra* means "wheel" or "disk" and connotes a vortex of energy, and in nature and function they are far more complex than the physical centers with which they are associated.

The stimulation of these *chakras* produces changes in consciousness which affect one's mental, moral and vital qualities. It also heightens one's awareness beyond the greatest capacity of rational comprehension. Consequently, when the *kundalini* rises, one's body, temperament and character undergo a metamorphosis, culminating eventually in an expanded creative consciousness when it reaches the upper source of the nectar— union with God, *samadhi*, the state of total self-fulfillment.

In this brief essay it is not possible to do justice to either the Book of Revelation or to the yoga counterparts of the experience it describes. Therefore, we will not attempt to give more than a partial summary in order to underscore the similarities between the writings.

Often in manuals of spiritual development,

meditation is presented as a reasoned application of the mind upon some great spiritual truth in order to penetrate its meaning and to increase fondness for it. Certainly one may devote mental energies in this direction with profit, but this procedure is not the type of meditation that will lead one to the deeper realms of inner awareness where the Christ-consciousness awaits. This comes from non-discoursive meditation, the method known in raja yoga as *dhyana*, and it is such an experience that John describes in Revelation.

John's Revelation records the spiritual odyssey of Self-realization which is the aim of all religions, but its credibility can be established only gradually through one's own inner experience. No outer, or objective, evidence could corroborate the inner truth which John experiences, but he is a candidate for the highest initiation; his vision of the Logos reveals his own spiritual self. Just as Jesus had attained the Christ-consciousness, so now the same paradigm of Self-realization is manifested in John: through meditation, John is led to a regeneration of self, a rebirth, a dying to the old self and an awakening to new life.

In Revelation, then, John traces the development of his self-discovery in an allegory of seven centers, or cities. The Greek word for church means *purposeful assembly*, and the seven churches, or communities of which John is writing coincide with the seven principle ganglia of the human body and to the seven *chakras* described in tantric yoga. They are also the seven lampstands, the light, or fields of consciousness, that he depicts as awakening in sequence, and they are the seven seals which interpenetrate the outer, or gross, physical body. Passing through these centers effects a startling metamorphosis in him, for great powers are contained in them. So he carefully mentions the consequences of abusing as well as the rewards to be derived from these energizing powers, lest the initiate naively expect automatic success.

John notes that when he hears a trumpet sound, a vision accompanies it. The ancient Sanskrit texts, too, note that the simultaneity of sight and sound has a physiological basis, and that when the *chakras* are stimulated, meditational awareness often includes definite sounds and colors.

But however fascinating each of these levels of new awareness may be, John must travel further in search of the fullness of divine grace within, for his self, as the image and likeness of God, is emerging into conscious awareness.

Revelation 2:1 to 3:22 gives a graphic description of the various city-churches which occupy John's attention. His concern for the welfare of these churches occasions the writing of a letter to each of them in which he delivers various kinds of instruction, veiled in highly symbolic terms, to the particular "angel" who receives the letter. He then continues his inner odyssey and describes how he was brought face-to-face with a sacred scroll that bore seven seals. A special "lamb" undertook the breaking of these seals, and with the breaking of each John experiences further visions. Finally the last seal is severed, but instead of a culminating revelation, John experiences only silence.

This entire sequence baffles the scholar as well as the lay reader. Attempts have been made to interpret the symbols by correlating them to the current events of the day, the impending fall of the decaying Roman Empire, foretelling in grotesque fashion its immanent destruction. But at the same time there are recurring themes and figures of speech that one easily recognizes from the earlier gospels.

For those who are familiar with the ancient texts describing the evolution of spiritual growth from the perspective of consciousness, these Christian symbols bear an uncanny resemblance to those found in the older writings in terms of their colors, sounds and shapes as well as the sequence in which they appear. One can find parallels to them also in the various Books of the Dead that have been translated into English.

What we are suggesting here is that this remarkable narrative of John could have not only a historical basis, but also—and this is crucially important—a fundamentally spiritual one as well, but one whose reality is heavily veiled in the language of symbol.

John, in other words, is experiencing the Christ-consciousness in Revelation; his narrative is an attempt to condense the various levels of its awakening into the language of symbol. In his own way he is confirming its universal message by associating it with the inner transformation of his being.

While many of the Eastern commentaries dwell at great length upon the subtle intricacies of the physical and mental transformations that take place as the energy moves upward, John's short presentation covers only the barest outline. His limited descriptions should be filled in by the aspirant's own experience in meditation, for everyone must learn for himself the process of self-conquest and experience personally the new birth of oneself as a spiritual being. Each one, as a sacrificial lamb, must liberate the *chakras* and acquire the spiritual prizes.

The most startling insight to be gained from comparing the tantric texts with the Book of Revelation is their mutual agreement that *dhyana*, or meditation, can eventually lead to a direct experience of God. If this is correct, then a number of problem areas intrinsic to institutionalized Christianity are eliminated. For one thing, intuition, or the direct experience of spiritual truth, supplants dogma, or belief, as the basis of religion. The merely tentative security of formal beliefs yields to the real knowledge of divine realities. Faith is necessary only to the extent that one accept the hypothesis that it is possible to come to the ultimately real through the meditational method. Thus, the experiential process dispenses with the insecurity of authoritative religion, and faith is replaced by conviction. Reaching the higher levels of consciousness and witnessing reality for oneself leads the true disciple far beyond the disillusionment that frequently separates Christian sectarians.

Though the method whereby one acquires an understanding of John's Revelation may disturb some Western Christians, it is only by patient self-exposure to the path of meditation that the aspiring knower will really attain high wisdom. Intellectual assent to religious truths will not earn salvation. Faith in the possibilities shown in Revelation may launch the adventure of meditation, but even faith cannot provide the experience that leads to total rebirth. Only by transcending faith and reason, both of which are based in finite experience, and by practicing meditation can one begin to grasp the significance of Self-realization in Christ-consciousness. The greatest of Christian leaders are those who demonstrate the fruits of Self-realization in their own lives and induce in others a similar experience.

As scientific research in the areas of biofeedback and the resulting conscious extension of human volition over the autonomic systems continues, a wider understanding of human potentiality results. We are beginning to learn that man, in his body, mind and spirit, is more endowed than previously suspected, and these scientific probings will definitely have their impact upon man as a religious being. In other words, the continuing comparing of ancient texts with modern laboratory findings can shed new light upon the ancient wisdom that grounds a true religious belief in the destiny of man.

Hesychasm and the Origins of Christian Meditative Discipline

Father William Teska

The beginnings of Christian meditative discipline are very early, going back to the very origin of Christian monasticism in the third century in the desert of Egypt, and continuing over the centuries to their flowering in many places. The tradition flowered, in particular, in northern Greece during the Byzantine Empire, especially at Mount Athos. There, a school of meditation, known as Hesychasm, developed between the tenth and fourteenth centuries and continues down to the present day.

It is interesting for our purposes to note that the development of Christian meditative disciplines should have begun in Egypt because much of the intellectual, philosophical, and theological basis of the practice of meditation in Christianity also comes out of the theology of Hellenic and Roman Egypt. This is significant because it was in Alexandria that Christian theology had the most contact with the various gnostic speculations which, according to many scholars, have their roots in the East, possibly in India.

There are many similarities between the systems of theology found in India and the various gnostic systems of theology, some Christian and some non-Christian, which flourished, especially in Egypt, before and shortly after the time of Christ. The idea of the transmigration of souls, for example, has an analogue in gnostic speculations originating in Greek thought. This concept was known in Pythagorean philosophy as metempsychosis, and it was absorbed by the greatest theologian of the ancient Church between St. Paul and St. Augustine—Origen of Alexandria.

Origen, who died in 255 A.D., was part of the Catechetical school in Egypt. His teacher was Clement, and Clement's teacher was a mysterious figure called Pantaenus who, according to Coptic legend, spent a good deal of his time in India. In addition to his training in this tradition, Origen had close contact with the original Christian monks in the desert outside of Alexandria. Thus, even though scholarship has yet to establish a definite link between gnosticism and ancient Indian Brahmanism, there may be such a connection because Origen's system of Christian theology drew heavily upon the gnostic traditions which were current in Egypt at his time, and many of his thoughts—indeed, his whole world view—bear striking resemblance to some of the major ideas of Hindu theology.

While it would be dangerous to assume too easily that Christianity assimilated many Hindu traditions in the manner just described, yet it is certain that the birthplace of Christian monasticism and the contemplative tradition (that is,

Egypt) was also the home of those systems of Christian theology which bore the closest resemblance to Indian systems. It was in Egypt, for example, that ascetic discipline first arose in the Church (*ascesis* in Greek simply means training, athletic training as for a contest). St. Paul had already used the athletic analogy when he spoke of the Christian life as a race, and the ancient monks understood asceticism to be a very palpable type of training, physical as well as spiritual, which was best undertaken alone in the desert.

After a century or so there arose among the ascetic monks the tradition of seeking the guidance of certain spiritual fathers, analogous to masters or *gurus,* for it had become clear, in the development of ascetic practice, that total solitude, starting from the beginning of one's spiritual struggle, could sometimes be destructive and even diabolical. For this reason one of the greatest early ascetic theologians of the Christian East, John Klimakos, issued a very stern warning to those who would embark on a life of spiritual training or ascesis and he insisted that the first step in such a discipline was to find a spiritual father and to place oneself entirely under his guidance.

Before continuing with the description of the development of ascetic theology, it would be helpful at this point to say a few words about church history, because Americans have at best a very foggy notion about forms of Christianity other than Protestantism. Most of us, for instance, have heard of the Greek Orthodox Church or the Russian Orthodox Church, but very few of us know much about the ancient roots of the tradition. We think of Christianity as the Bible-oriented social institution which finds its expression in the numerous Protestant denominations existing in the United States, but this form of Christianity is only a small part of the whole. It is, as it were, merely a small twig on the branch of the trunk of the whole tree which is the Christian church, and this is something quite different indeed from the type of Christianity of which we speak when we talk about the monks of ancient Egypt. This is important to note because the practices of contemplation and meditation in which we are interested were developed primarily and were most important in the Christian East.

There were in the ancient world five great centers of Christianity: Rome, Antioch, Alexandria, Constantinople, and Jerusalem, and each of these cities was the See of a patriarch, the chief bishop of the church in that part of the world. It is not our purpose here to investigate the historical and theological causes for the fact that during the Middle Ages the four Eastern patriarchs (Antioch, Alexandria, Constantinople and Jerusalem) became increasingly estranged from the patriarch of Rome and eventually lost all communication with him; a convenient date for this split, long honored by historians is, 1054 A.D.

when the Pope excommunicated the patriarch of Constantinople and the patriarch of Constantinople excommunicated the Pope.

But the division started long before that with the breakdown of communication that ensued after the Gothic invasions of the Western empire. One result of this breakdown is still with us, and that is the fact that we Westerners have become extremely chauvinistic in that we know almost nothing of the development of anything in Byzantium, including Christianity. But it was there in Byzantium that the ascetic life was emphasized and the spiritual and contemplative life was developed, while in the West the emphasis quickly came to be more rational and scientific, beginning with the development of scholasticism in the twelfth and thirteenth centuries.

It is interesting to note that about the same time the scholastic movement was laying the foundations of Western science in the West, the monks of the East were beginning to develop the practice known as Hesychasm, which is remarkably similar to yoga in many ways. It was developed as a result of a long, long line of teachers (not necessarily in a direct master-disciple relationship, although there were long periods in which this was the case). Unfortunately, however, we have no reliable historical information as to the length of the continuity of such lines of masters and teachers, yet it is certain that such lines did exist, and it is interesting to notice the similarity here with Indian tradition.

It would be a great mistake to draw too many analogies between Hesychast and yoga practices, but there are, nevertheless, similarities, however superficial they may be. We know, for example, that there were periods of several centuries in which the teaching of ascetic practice passed from spiritual father to disciple, as is the case with yoga. This started in the Egyptian desert and continues to the present day, although it is often impossible to trace the succession of masters and disciples with historical accuracy. Monasteries dissolved, there were great upheavals in society, some of the practices were lost, and the tradition has not been so evenly preserved as has the tradition of yoga. But even so, tradition still exists in Christianity, and it is preserved in writing and in various other forms. There are still Hesychasts in the holy mountain (Athos), and in Soviet Russia.

As mentioned above, Christian meditative discipline began in ancient Egypt, and the experience of the fathers of the desert, as they are called, plays to this day an essential part in the training of Christian ascetics. (The Eastern Hesychasts, especially, view the fathers of the desert and their successors over the centuries with great reverence). The first and foremost of these was the famous Anthony. Everyone has at some time seen a painting of the temptations of St. Anthony, for this motif depicts Anthony in his warfare against spiritual adversaries, a favorite theme of medieval artists. Many other fountainheads of Christian ascetic practice could also be named here, but among the most important were Dionysius, the pseudo-Areopagite, who wrote the first treatise on mystical theology, and St. John Klimakos, mentioned above. *Klimakos* simply means ladder, and John is so named because of his treatise on ascetic theology called *The Ladder of Divine Ascent* in which he enumerated thirty-three stages (steps on the ladder) in the progress of the soul into oneness with the Godhead.

The goal of all of the ascetic and mystical practices of Christianity was, for the ancients, nothing less than divinization. This word is seldom used in Western Christianity, but it was very important in Hellenic and Eastern Christianity. The same word in Greek is *apotheosis*, and it means, becoming one with God in an ineffable and mysterious way. Origen speaks of it, and it was so important to the fathers of the ancient church that when the church found it necessary to entertain a new doctrine or a new theological system, the question would always be raised, "Does this new teaching allow for apotheosis or not? Does it allow for humanity to become one with God?" If the new doctrine did not allow for apotheosis, it was treated with great suspicion; if it did, it was entertained. Thus, apotheosis was the ideal in ancient Eastern theology as well as the goal of ascetic discipline. Theologians such as

Dionysius, the pseudo-Areopagite, and John Klimakos pursued this quest of apotheosis as did all subsequent Byzantine theologians of any importance. St. Simeon Stylites, for instance, St. Maximus the Confessor and St. John of Damascus were all practicing ascetics, pursuing the quest of apotheosis, and this tradition continued right down to the tenth century when Hesychasm began to be important as a school of meditation.

The first great exponent of this school was a theologian named St. Simeon Neotheologos, who was so highly regarded in the East that he was called, the "New Theologian" (the "First Theologian" was St. John the Divine, the writer of the Fourth Gospel and the Apocalypse), and he is famous for having written a series of instructions to Hesychasts on the subject of mental quiet. (*Hesychia* in Greek simply means "quiet," and Hesychasm is the practice of developing this interior calm and quiet with a specific end in mind—that of apotheosis, or becoming one with God.)

Many of Simeon's instructions to Hesychasts, or those who were embarked on a life of the practice of mental quiet, are interesting because of the comparisons that can be made between them and yogic discipline. They included physical exercises (as in hatha yoga) and certain meditative postures—one of which involved sitting with the back straight and with the beard pressed against the sternum, the eyes fixed upon the abdomen.

This posture gave rise to the derogatory Latin term which has come into our own language in its English translation as "navel gazer." "Sit and contemplate your navel," people say, when speaking of meditation in a derogatory way. (This was a term that the Jesuits invented for the Hesychasts because of the posture described above.) But one of the purposes of this posture is to try to fix one's attention on the location of the heart, first to become aware of the heartbeat and then to find within the breast the location of the heart. At the same time, according to Hesychasm, one's breathing is to become slow and regular, and the well-known Jesus Prayer is to be repeated many, many times like a mantra.

It is because of the importance of the heart that the discipline of Hesychasm and the particular prayer, "Lord Jesus Christ, Son of God, have mercy upon me" have become known as Prayer of the Heart. Hesychast theoreticians held that by concentrating on the heart and by breathing in a regular way (as taught by the master to the disciple) and at the same time by repeating the prayer of Jesus (or some other prayer assigned by the spiritual father), the soul could progress to ever-higher stages of consciousness and sanctity until at last it was enabled to perceive the radiance of the God-head immediately, directly, and fully. Such a vision, of course, can be recognized as a description of the ancient goal of apotheosis, and the Hesychasts had developed what they considered to be a methodical practice to prepare oneself for this apotheosis.

The practice of Hesychasm flourished mainly at a place called Mount Athos, located east of Thessalonika and west of Constantinople, which is probably the most important center of Christian spirituality since the Egyptian desert. Mount Athos, also called simply the Holy Mountain, has been a center of Christian monasticism since the ninth century, and no woman has set foot on it since that time. There are at present some twenty-eight to thirty active monasteries—Greek, Russian, Serbian, Syrian, and so on—on the holy mountain, even though it must be recognized that it is not what it once was, and there are signs of apparent decline. There were at one time, for instance, Russian monasteries built there by the imperial family in the nineteenth century, and some of the largest monasteries, called *lavras*, were, in fact, small cities that held up to three thousand monks. Almost all of these were Hesychasts.

A controversy arose during the centuries that followed the work of St. Simeon, the "New Theologian," and it culminated in the fourteenth century with the work of the great theologian, St. Gregory of Palamas. The basic question of the controversy was whether or not it is possible for a created being to perceive, without meditation, the essence of the Godhead. Could a human being, imprisoned in the body, hope to perceive the un-created light, the light which surrounded our

Lord when He was transfigured before the apostles on Mount Tabor? Could, in other words, a human being really hope to achieve apotheosis? The Hesychast party, of course, said Yes, it could be done through the discipline of asceticism and mental quiet, that is—the disciplines of Hesychasm. The opposing party, whose intellectual leader was a certain Barlaam of Calabria, held that such a vision of God is impossible for human beings. The controversy raged, and at one point St. Gregory was deposed and imprisoned, but finally he was reinstated and made the Bishop of Thessalonika. Finally, the Hesychast party won the theological issue, and a special feast was dedicated in the Orthodox Church in honor of this victory. One may see the symbol of this victory of Hesychasm in the habit of any Orthodox monk even to this day, for on his hand he wears a string of beads, much like a rosary, which is used for counting the number of Jesus Prayers that he says under the direction of his spiritual father.

The practice of Hesychasm on Mount Athos continued up until the beginning of the nineteenth century when large numbers of Russian monks started to arrive on the holy mountain. Then from Mount Athos, the practice of Hesychasm was carried back to Russia. Those who have read *Frannie and Zooey,* by J. D. Salinger, have heard of the remarkable book called *The Way of the Pilgrim*, written by an anonymous Russian peasant in the nineteenth century. In it he describes his

journey through Russia during which he encounters a Hesychast monk who teaches him to
say the Jesus Prayer and gives him certain other
exercises. With that alone, the pilgrim embarks on
a life of prayer and mental quiet.

There were many such pilgrims and holy men
in Russia in the nineteenth century when asceticism was still very strong, and some of the most
powerful of these Hesychasts became known as
startsi, or elders. These holy men lived in all parts
of Russia (some even came to Alaska and introduced the practice to American soil), and many of
them had large followings, sometimes numbered
in the hundreds of thousands. Even as late as the
1930's there was a famous *starets* living on Mount
Athos who wrote about his own spiritual pilgrim-
age, and whose life was a fine example of Eastern
piety, in particular, of Hesychasm.

The Russian revolution forced a great many
vital spiritual traditions underground. Even so, although it is very difficult to say with any certainty
whether the tradition of Hesychasm is still strong
in Russia, it may be assumed that there are still
practitioners because Hesychasm played such an
important role in Russian spirituality at its deepest
level. On Mount Athos there are still hermits and
ascetics, some of whom live in caves and who can
be visited only by climbing up chains to the part
of the cliff in which they live. They hardly ever
see anyone, but it is more than likely that they
still practice the ancient disciplines.

Yoga, Meditation and Christianity

Pandit Usharbudh Arya, Ph.D.

Yoga, in the last few decades, has become a household word, and the practice of meditation has been gaining an increasing popularity. But in some quarters there are questions as to whether yoga and meditation fit with the doctrines of Christianity. Every now and then one encounters a certain amount of scepticism as to whether or not yoga meditation is compatible with Christian practices, especially among the very orthodox people of the West. This essay is therefore designed to help answer such questions as they relate to the meditative tradition in Christianity.

It must be remembered that Christianity, like all religions, has its roots in the East, so a study of the history of Christian doctrine should not be made in isolation from the history of general Eastern thought. Even though Christianity is today regarded as a distinctly Western doctrine, its Eastern orientation cannot be altogether suppressed. Christ still wears the robes of His land, and it is even possible that He might be denied entry into a modern hotel if He were to appear in downtown New York today.

Cultures develop strange prejudices and

reactions to things which appear alien to them. Yet they cannot exist separately from each other, and a great deal of mutual appreciation and assimilation goes on unconsciously. No one in the West today, for instance, resents the use of the decimal or of Indian numerals. The use of calico and chintz was not discouraged because they were imported from India. Karate and judo are accepted as genuine sciences. Similarly, in the Eastern countries radio, tight pants, television and the necktie have become commonplace. This type of mutual exchange among cultures has been going on for many thousands of years, including the period before and during the time of Christ. By the same token, even though it is Eastern in origin, meditation is not a non-Christian teaching; through meditation, true Christianity shares with the rest of the Eastern religions a seeking for God within and an aspiration to realize the true nature of the divine spark which is man.

If we look carefully at the history of ancient cultures we will find that such teachings continually flowed into the mainstream of early Christianity. One of the earliest examples of the Indian influence in Western philosophy, for instance, is to be found in the teaching of Pythagoras who is regarded as the father of Greek philosophy. Then, if you read the fifteenth chapter of the *Metamorphoses* of Ovid, the famous Latin poet, you will find there Pythagoras' teachings concerning reincarnation, vegetarianism and meditational experiences—in verses that are almost identical to those of ancient Hindu scriptures. The reason for this is that Pythagoras, who rebelled against the tyranny of the rulers of his island, Samos, went eastward and studied there for many years before returning to Greece and establishing the first academy of philosophy in the West along patterns similar to those of an ancient *ashram*. The same rules of discipline and initiations were observed; the same philosophy of compassion toward all living beings was taught. And through Pythagoras these teachings spread to the West.

Such schools of philosophy, under the guidance of great teachers, continued throughout Greek history until they were closed by the orders of later Roman emperors. (It should be remembered that Pythagoras was a contemporary of the Buddha.) The philosophy of Socrates is thus recognized as bearing a strong resemblance to many of the teachings in the Upanishads. His emphasis on the incompleteness of sense experiences and on a higher reality behind appearances is nothing but the deepest Upanishadic philosophy. Once again, his dialogues on reincarnation as well as his own personal life (as described by Xenophon) bear testimony to some direct or indirect influence from the East.

The disciple of Socrates, Aristotle, was the teacher of Alexander of Macedonia who conquered many countries and finally invaded northwestern India. Then, while Alexander was in

India, he came into contact with Indian philosophers, and both Plutarch and Pliny referred to Alexander's contact with these sages of India and to the fact that he brought some of them back to the West with him. Plutarch, in his *Lives*, calls these philosophers "gymnosophists," but gymnosophists are none other than yogis, wise men who also practiced many physical exercises.

Then we come to the third century B.C. when the Emperor Ashoka ruled over a vast empire in India. Scholars have dug up inscriptions, known as the Edicts of Ashoka, declaring his philosophy and containing his advice to his subjects and these bear a marked resemblance to some of the teachings of Christ. That there was a cultural interchange between East and West is very possible because Ashoka exchanged ambassadors with the Ptolemies of Egypt and also sent Buddhist monks to establish monasteries in Syria. These Buddhist monasteries were still flourishing in the time of Christ.

Christ's mother tongue was Aramaic. Ashoka's inscriptions of three centuries before Christ were also in Aramaic, thus suggesting, on purely scholarly evidence, that the possibility of Christ's own contact with India cannot be ruled out.

In addition, many passages of the Old Testament are identical to those of the Upanishads. For example, God says to Moses that his name is, "I am" or "I am that I am," which is the formula *soham*, used in many yoga meditations and found in the *Vedas* at approximately 3000 B.C.

Who were the *magi* who visited Christ at His birth? Are they possibly the teachers of the doctrine of *maya* in Vedanta philosophy? The word cannot be explained in any other way.

The yogis of the Himalayas often say that Christ studied with them until the age of thirty, and there can be no argument with the fact that the baptism of Christ was identical to the initiations into the monastic life given among Buddhists and Hindus a thousand years before Christ. For three or four thousand years, as a matter of fact, monks of the swami orders have been introduced into monastic orders by taking a dip in the river, after which the initiating monk hands a rough robe to the new monk and blesses him by placing his hand on the initiate's head. The sentence in the Bible, "And the Holy Ghost descended like a dove," and the present custom in the Christian church of ordaining a priest by the bishop's placing his hand on the new priest's head are vestiges of ritual practices whose inner purpose is no longer understood. In yoga, however, such high initiations, whereby the guru's expanded consciousness is passed on to the disciple, are known and still alive in the Himalayan tradition.

The powers of yoga are so well known to the tradition of India that when the Hindu today reads the life story of Christ, his reaction to all the miracles described is that they are the *siddhis*, the spiritual accomplishments whereby the forces of nature are controlled. The miracle of walking on water is also mentioned in Buddhist scriptures. Many of the parables, such as that of the Prodigal Son, have also been traced to the same Buddhist texts.

In both the Jewish and the Western tradition one stands to preach, whereas in the Buddhist and the Hindu tradition a teacher sits. Christ sat to preach the Sermon on the Mount. Sentences like, "I am the Way and the Truth and the Life" seem to echo the statements of Krishna in the *Bhagavad Gita.* And long before St. John's Gospel the Sanskrit grammarians were writing of *Shabda-Brahman*, "the word that is God," for, according to the Vedic tradition, all Word was regarded as revelation; all teaching and inspiration as well as the whole universe originated from the principle of the mystic sound.

Saul, later St. Paul, on his way to Damascus was not struck blind; he passed through a very high yogic initiation in which his eyes were closed by force so that he might see only the inner light.

It should also be remembered that some of the Christian meditative traditions have been traced back to Ethiopia and Egypt. Both countries had a continuous exchange of sages and mystics from India where the yoga philosophy had matured long before this time. Thus, the philosophy of the Upanishads and yoga continued to strengthen the mystic stream of Christianity long after Christ. Scholars have also established, without a doubt, that the neoplatonic school of Christianity owes a direct or indirect debt to the philosophy of the Upanishads.

In the Jewish tradition several sects followed a discipline that closely resembled those of the Hindu and Buddhist monasteries. What is more, the disciplines followed in the Roman Catholic monasteries today are very similar to those of the ancient Indian monasteries. Even though the dictionaries trace the origin of the word *monk* to the Greek *monos*, meaning "alone," I am of the opinion that its roots might go back to the Sanskrit *muni*, meaning "monk." The word *muni* occurs in this sense for the first time in a hymn in the *Rig-Veda* (1500 B.C.) in which the way of the lone hermits, who have withdrawn from the villages to forests and to a life of wandering, is extolled.

In this connection, observe also the following: the English word *man* has its origin in the Sanskrit verb root *man*, which means, "to think, to meditate." The Sanskrit *manas* is "mind" (Latin *mens*), the instrument of thought and meditation. *Manu* is the first man, the first lawgiver, the personified *mantra. Mantra* (also *manu*) is a sound vibration introduced by a *guru* into the disciple's mind to make it a vehicle for meditation. *Muni* is a monk, hermit or mendicant silently meditating with a mantra. *Mauna* is silence, the disposition of a *muni*. All of these words originate in the same root which means, "to meditate." It is not possible that a monastic tradition could develop outside of the chain of concepts expressed by the single root *man*.

From the third century B.C. to the time of Christ the trade between India and ancient Rome could not have failed to introduce Indian ideas of metaphysics along with silk, spices, ivory, and even some styles in sculpture. This trade continued through Byzantium and later through Venice. Is it possible that those who brought the decimal and the Indian numerals did not speak of the motivation of Indian life, the spiritual aspiration to unite with God?

Academicians have shown that *Aesop's Fables* and the stories of Andersen and the brothers Grimm owe their existence to the rich literature of India, especially to the *Panchatantra*, the *Jatakas*, and many other voluminous texts. The theme of the pound of flesh in *The Merchant of Venice* has been traced to the *Shivijataka*, one of the stories of the former lives of the Buddha. The story of *A Comedy of Errors* is in the same way a borrowing from a similar story found in the Sanskrit, *Ocean of Story, Katha-saritsagara*.

Some of the yoga doctrines became thoroughly distorted through this long journey from India to Elizabethan England. Take, for example, the fairies in *A Midsummer Night's Dream*. Shakespeare speaks of their homeland having been in India, and that they lived in flowers. Now, the word "fairy" is derived from the Iranian *pari*, which in turn is derived from the Sanskrit word *apsaras*, the celestial, semi-divine beings who gamboled on water at night, exactly the picture one has of the fairies from Shakespeare's drama. The *devis*, divine mothers representing the forces of consciousness, reside in the lotuses of the seven centers of consciousness. They have no weight or volume, nor do the fairies, but a reader of *A Midsummer Night's Dream* today will not easily recognize this remote connection of the fairies with the *chakras* of yoga meditation.

Now we come to the modern period. Goethe's praise of the Sanskrit drama, Schopenhauer's reinterpretation of the philosophy of the Upanishads (however pessimistic), Hegel's paraphrases of some of the *Sankhya* doctrine—all of these are enough to prove that the mystic philosophy of India was introduced into the West long before its recent renaissance.

The very foundations of American intellectualism are in Thoreau and Emerson, both avid readers of the Bhagavad Gita and the Upanishads. Emerson's concept of the Oversoul and his translation of some of the passages of the Upanishads are well known. His poem on Brahman, "If the red slayer thinks he slays and the slain thinks he is slain . . . " is a translation from the Bhagavad Gita and *The Katha Upanishad*. And Thoreau and Emerson were not isolated thinkers. They were in the mainstream of transcendentalist writers of the time and were thus a strong influence on American culture.

We have given this historical outline in the attempt to show that what is being absorbed in American thought today from Eastern teachings is neither something completely new nor quite alien. The cultures of the East and the West have always borrowed from one another and will continue to. The present trend of bringing the spiritual teachings from the East to the West and the material sciences from the West to the East points to a very healthy future for our planet.

The meditative tradition has come to America not only via this East-to-West route, but also across the Pacific. This will be seen in the history of the word *zen.* The yoga word for meditation in Sanskrit is *dhyana* which in Pali, the Buddha's spoken language, became *jhana.* The Indian Buddhist monks took the word to China where it was pronounced, *ch'an.* The Chinese and the Koreans then brought it to Japan where it became *zen*, and finally the Japanese sugar estate workers in Hawaii introduced it to California. This journey of *dhyana* or *zen* from India to America took approximately two thousand years (there is nothing in *zen* that is not known to yoga, but there is much in yoga that is not known to *zen*). It must be credited with having aroused a great deal of scientific curiosity in the United States, leading to the laboratory tests pioneered by men like Kamiya on the brainwaves of monks in meditation. Modern biofeedback techniques were the natural outcome of this.

The unfortunate part of the story of the spread of meditative philosophy in the West, however, is that it has, without fail, lost touch with its sources of grace and the original teachings, and each time a teacher comes he has to break fresh ground. It is for this reason that the West has never produced worthy successors to the Masters of the Himalayas (except when some highly evolved Westerners make the Himalayas their home). Each time a little bit of the teaching has been introduced it has been mistaken for the whole, and the spiritually young began to play the *guru*. For instance, the rosary and the repetition of prayer have been retained, but the higher consciousness of *mantra* has been lost. A small part of the Eastern healing technique, learned by Mesmer, became hypnotism (which is wrongly equated with meditation). Biofeedback research acknowledges scant debt to yoga in little footnotes because each researcher is anxious to proclaim the greatness of his own genius and "discovery." That would be perfectly all right if it did not fill people with false ego which blocks the further flow of grace as well as the teachings from the great Masters. Even more unfortunate is the *guru-droha* of some Westernized teachers of India.

It should also be remembered that there is much in the history, doctrine and practice of Christianity which is of the East, and more wisdom would have kept replenishing this reservoir if ego had not intervened and placed unnecessary obstacles in the way. For this reason all yoga meditation begins with the formula *gurubhyo namah*, "obeisance to the gurus," may their grace bless this meditation.

We have briefly referred to the similarities between the Bible and the Upanishads. These similarities can also be found in the later meditative stream of Christianity. The doctrine of apotheosis, for instance, reminds one of the Upanishadic passage *Brahma veda brahmaiva bhavati*, "He who knows Brahman becomes Brahman." To be totally absorbed in one's deity, to lose the identity of the ego, to become one with the *ishta devata* (one's chosen deity), is an essential part of the Indian doctrine of *bhakti*, the path of emotional devotion to God. To a yogi of India, Christ can be one's chosen deity, and has been with at least some of them.

What is the difference between meditation as practiced in Christian monasteries today and the yoga technique? Unfortunately, the deeper meditative tradition has been lost in these monasteries. The paths of an inward journey through the mazes of the mind into the deepest *sanctum sanctorum* of the divine heart have been forgotten. Mary is just a semi-human, semi-divine figure and no longer the Virgin Mother residing within all of us. Christ of the Sacred Heart exists only in icons and pictures.

Meditation as taught to an average Catholic monk is what a yogi would term an act of contemplation. It is more in the nature of *jnana yoga,* the yoga of knowledge, in which a sentence of very high significance is taken, studied, examined, thought about, and absorbed into one's personality. But beyond such contemplation are the higher states of meditation, the levels of *samadhi,* in which such discursive thought and the words which are the vehicle of such thought are transcended, in which thinker, thinking, thought and the vehicle of thought merge into one reality of supreme consciousness. This science of apotheosis, *Brahma-bhava,* has been lost and needs to be revived if Christianity is once again to become the source of inspiration that it once was.

What is the difference between the experiences of the Christian mystics and the yogis of the Himalayas? The narratives of the lives of Christian mystics indicate an emotional joy in union and pain and crying and weeping when separated from the love of God. Such experiences come under the category of bhakti yoga, which is the uplifting of all emotions in surrender to the sublime. It is the yoga of the lover and the beloved. It is the song of the union of Radha and Krishna. It is the poem of the mystic-sage-poetess Meera, in the sixteenth century of India, and of the blind singer-saint-mystic Suradasa, who composed and sang ten thousand songs of devotion to Krishna. (It is said that the child Krishna would come and sit before Suradasa to listen to these offerings.

A mystic's absorption in the joyful experience of God is the *samprajnata samadhi*, the meditation in which an object remains. Such a meditation may be accompanied with thoughts, with ecstasy, and one's own sense of separate self-existence. This is the case with the states attained by many mystics, both of India and the West. A yogi, however, is far beyond the state of being a mystic, for mysticism is only a step toward the highest *samadhi* (the experience of becoming one with the totality of the supreme consciousness of God). In such a state the expression of ecstasy known to the mystics no longer exists; these are left behind for the *bhaktas*.

Christianity is primarily a religion of *bhakti*, of total self-surrender, and it is this *bhakti* that appeals to the India of today to such an extent that no Indian of whatever faith can fail to cry when reading the Sermon on the Mount from the Gospel according to St. Matthew. But unfortunately, the Western Christian of today regards it against his dignity to shed a tear in devotion and surrender. Instead, he splits the hairs of theology; he has changed the religion of *bhakti* into a religion of *jnana*; he has made religion an intellectual pursuit which examines doctrine with the thoroughness of a logician—but without making it a personal experience of God.

Those who are interested in true Christian

meditation should understand the figures of the Mother Mary and the Christ of the Sacred Heart, so the first steps in the technique of Christian meditation would be as follows:

Perform a relaxation exercise in the corpse posture.

Sit up on your meditation seat, and after doing the basic breathing exercises and channel purification, visualize your *ishta devata*, the chosen deity, Mother Mary, or Christ of the Sacred Heart.

Visualize this chosen deity in the space of the psychic heart, the cardiac plexus, or the depression above the stomach, below the chest, in the center.

The figure of your deity is radiant with light, sending out the rays of purest white divine light in all directions into your personality surrounding your own physical figure with the same aura of the purest white divine light.

Breathe slowly, gently and completely.

With each breath recite a prayer. If the figure is Mary, then recite "Hail Mary" with each exhalation and again with the inhalation.

If the figure is of Jesus, recite the name Jesus or some other brief prayer such as:

> Lord Jesus Christ,
>   have mercy upon my soul
> Hallowed by Thy name
> Let there be light
> I am that I am

or other such *mantras*.

Some of the sentences may be divided into two, between exhalation and inhalation.

There should be no pause between the exhalation and inhalation.

Do not recite with your mouth, and do not move your tongue.

With each inhalation let the prayer go deep into your mind. Who is it that recites the prayer? Where is that divine spark from which all prayers are inspired? Go into the depths of your mind, holding on to the string of your breath, like entering into the depths of a cave in the center of which a divine spark burns.

Repeat the same prayer, and no other, at your meditation time and while walking, driving, sitting, cooking, having sexual intercourse, or falling asleep.

Do so until the prayer becomes a habit of your consciousness and it is remembered even when you faintly wake during your sleep.

When you have reached that point in your progress, ask your spiritual teacher for further instructions.

Whatever meditation you do, a spiritual instructor, a *guru*, is absolutely necessary. Those who have opened themselves up to *chit-shakti*, the Holy Ghost, have been graced with divine light and are the vehicles of this light; it is through their hands, their prayers, their grace, their saintly intercession that the Holy Ghost descends into your soul. However, just about the time that Christianity was Romanized it lost touch with its spiritual sources in the East, and as a result grace and the blessings of the Holy Ghost through the *gurus* seems to have ceased. It is for this reason that even though a long chain of bishops has ordained hundreds of thousands of priests for hundreds of years, no divine experiences take place through these acts of ordaining.

In order to become true members of the Church of Christ a person must know not who Jesus was, but what Christ is. Christ, *Ishvara*, is the very personal force pervading this universe that guides and illuminates every aspirant. It is the very spirit of the *guru*. It is not an embodied person, but rather the force in which all individual beings are divine sparks, the *shakti* that has incarnated many times. As the consciousness of a finger is one with the consciousness of the person and cannot exist without that consciousness, without that unity, so the person also is a mere finger in the complete personality of Christ. It is in this way that he is a limb, a member of the spirit of Christ.

The purpose of Christian meditation will be to realize this unity of all personalities with the personality of Christ. The same also is the personality of Krishna or of any other divine incarnation. A reading of the ninth, tenth and eleventh chapters of the Bhagavad Gita will greatly enhance the reader's understanding of the principle of this one divine personality of the universe.

The Authors

Swami Rama, the founder and spiritual head of the Himalayan International Institute of Yoga Science and Philosophy, was ordained a monk at a very young age by a great sage of the Himalayas. At one time he held the highest spiritual post in India, that of the Shankaracharya of Karvirpitham, which he renounced in 1952 in order to fulfill his mission in the West. Pandit Usharbudh Arya is a disciple of Swami Rama. He is the spiritual teacher at the Center for Higher Consciousness in Minneapolis and serves on the faculty of the Himalayan Institute. Justin O'Brien, Ph.D., is a former professor of theological studies at Loyola University and is presently Coordinator of Graduate Programs and Educational Studies at the Himalayan Institute. Father William Teska is a chaplain at the University Episcopal Center at the University of Minnesota. The Rev. Lawrence Bouldin is a minister of the United Methodist Church.

HIMALAYAN INSTITUTE PUBLICATIONS

Living with the Himalayan Masters	Swami Rama
Yoga and Psychotherapy	Swami Rama, R. Ballentine,M.D. Swami Ajaya
Science of Breath	Swami Rama, R. Ballentine, M.D. A. Hymes, M.D.
Emotion to Enlightenment	Swami Rama, Swami Ajaya
Freedom from the Bondage of Karma	Swami Rama
Book of Wisdom	Swami Rama
Lectures on Yoga	Swami Rama
Life Here and Hereafter	Swami Rama
Marriage, Parenthood & Enlightenment	Swami Rama
A Practical Guide to Holistic Health	Swami Rama
Superconscious Meditation	Pandit Usharbudh Arya, Ph.D.
Philosophy of Hatha Yoga	Pandit Usharbudh Arya, Ph.D.
Meditation and the Art of Dying	Pandit Usharbudh Arya, Ph.D.
God	Pandit Usharbudh Arya, Ph.D.
Yoga Psychology	Swami Ajaya
Foundations, Eastern & Western Psychology	Swami Ajaya (ed)
Psychology East and West	Swami Ajaya (ed)
Meditational Therapy	Swami Ajaya (ed)
Diet and Nutrition	Rudolph Ballentine, M.D.
Joints and Glands Exercises	Rudolph Ballentine, M.D. (ed)
Yoga and Christianity	Justin O'Brien, Ph.D.
Science Studies Yoga	James Funderburk, Ph.D.
Homeopathic Remedies	Drs. Anderson, Buegel, Chernin
Hatha Yoga Manual I	Samskrti and Veda
Hatha Yoga Manual II	Samskrti and Judith Franks
Swami Rama of the Himalayas	L. K. Misra, Ph.D. (ed)
Philosophy of Death and Dying	M. V. Kamath
Practical Vedanta of Swami Rama Tirtha	Brandt Dayton (ed)
The Swami and Sam	Brandt Dayton
Sanskrit Without Tears	S. N. Agnihotri, Ph.D.
Theory and Practice of Meditation	Himalayan Institute
Inner Paths	Himalayan Institute
Meditation in Christianity	Himalayan Institute
Faces of Meditation	Himalayan Institute
Art and Science of Meditation	Himalayan Institute
Therapeutic Value of Yoga	Himalayan Institute
Chants from Eternity	Himalayan Institute
Spiritual Diary	Himalayan Institute
Thought for the Day	Himalayan Institute
Himalayan Mountain Cookery	Martha Ballentine
The Yoga Way Cookbook	Himalayan Institute